GIANTS OF THE SEA

A PORTRAIT OF THE ANIMAL WORLD

ANDREW CLEAVE

TODTRI

This book was designed and produced by TODTRI Book Publishers
P.O. Box 572, New York, NY 10116-0572 FAX: (212) 695-6984

Printed and bound in Korea

ISBN 1-57717-076-8

Author: Andrew Cleave

Publisher: Robert M. Tod
Editor: Edward Douglas
Assistant Editor: Amy Handy
Book Designer: Mark Weinberg
Typesetting: Command-O Design

PHOTO CREDITS
Photo Source/Page Number

Dembinsky Photo Associate
Marilyn Kazmers 10

Innerspace Visions
Tom Campbell 54 (top)
Brandon Cole 19, 21 (top), 22, 24–25
Mark Conlin 4 (top), 21 (bottom)
Bob Cranston 3, 5, 7 (top & bottom), 42, 49 (top)
Ben Cropp 48
David B. Fleetham 12, 29, 33, 52, 56–57, 61
Richard Herrmann 46 (top)
Paul Humann 50 (top)
Mike Johnson 63
Marilyn Kazmers 18, 27
Nikolas Konstantinou 6
Hiroya Minakuchi 28 (bottom)
Amos Nachoum 45
Doug Perrine 13, 14, 15 (top & bottom), 16 (top & bottom), 17, 20, 26, 31 (bottom),
32 (bottom), 36, 37, 44, 50 (bottom), 55, 58, 59, 60, 62, 64 (bottom), 65, 66, 68–69, 70
Doug Perrine/Hawaii Whale Research Foundation 30
Robert L. Pitman 28 (top)
Bruce Rasner 46 (bottom)
Jeff Rotman 53 (top)
Mark Ruth 23 (bottom)
Ron & Valerie Taylor 51
James D. Watt 8–9, 31 (top), 32 (top), 43 (bottom), 47, 49 (bottom), 53 (bottom), 54 (bottom), 64 (top), 71
Doc White 23 (top)

Picture Perfect
C. H. Gomersall/Nature Photographers 38
M. P. Harris/Nature Photographers 40–41
Joe McDonald 43 (top)
Paul Sterry 67
John Warden 34, 35

Tom Stack & Associates
David B. Fleetham 11
David Young 4 (bottom)

Frank S. Todd 39

INTRODUCTION

Exploiting the rich nutrients of the seabed, a gray whale feeds in brightly lit, shallow water. They prefer such waters, where they can scoop mud from the bottom and filter out their food, usually shrimp, worms, and shellfish.

In the distant past, the giants of the sea were often perceived as monsters intent on the destruction of ships and all who sailed in them. Some even came ashore, as recounted in Homer's Iliad, to kill people on the beaches. These beliefs began soon after humans first built ocean-going vessels. Strange marine animals were sighted that had never been seen before, inspiring tales of enormous creatures as large as or even larger than ships. No doubt details were exaggerated and enhanced in the narration of these stories, and the creatures grew in size and ferocity with each retelling.

Some accounts have become part of the folklore of ancient peoples; the myths of classical Greece are filled with tales of the sea god Poseidon and his realm. The Bible, too, has its share of references to the deep, most notably in such stories as Jonah and the whale and the parting of the Red Sea.

During the Middle Ages, as ships traveled farther from home, European sailors came back with fantastic stories of sea serpents and monsters they had encountered. Gradually though, as myth, superstition, and fantasy gave way to science, people began to realize that the life forms of the sea, including its giants, were even more complex and miraculous than anyone had imagined.

A blue shark feeds on krill, an abundant order of tiny, bright red shrimp. An important link in the food chain, krill sustain the baleen whales as well as other creatures.

The coelacanth, a large carnivorous fish of the oceans depths, was thought to exist only in the fossil records until discovered alive about sixty years ago. This ancient species can measure over 5 feet (1.5 meters) long and weigh about 160 pounds (72 kilograms).

Ocean Zones

Today the seas are regarded as a vital and integral part of the life of our planet. Indeed, we now understand that the whole basis of life on earth is affected by the oceans. The very climate is governed by the seas, and both our food and the air we breathe depend on a healthy marine environment.

Some of the complexities of the ocean, as well as the lives of the sea's giants, are made clearer by an understanding of the three levels, or zones, into which the ocean waters are divided.

The Surface of the Sea

At the ocean's surface the water is at its warmest. Because of the water's contact with the air, the surface has the highest levels of oxygen. The turbulence of the waves leads to a constant aeration of the sea's upper layers, enriching the water with the oxygen essential to the respiration of fish. This is also where light intensity is brightest, so plant growth is most abundant here.

Billions of microscopic organisms live at the surface. Microscopic plants, single-celled members of the algae family, use the bright light of the sun to trap energy and make food. They also utilize nutrient-bearing minerals swept up by ocean currents from deep ocean troughs. When conditions are suitable, algae can grow and multiply in great abundance, allowing the microscopic animals that feed on them to increase in number.

Some of these microscopic organisms move independently, but most drift at the mercy of wind and tides, which carry them great distances. These drifting organisms are collectively known as plankton. Tiny as they are, as a group they are of immense importance to the giants of the sea, who all in some way or another depend on them for food.

Such a wealth of available planktonic food results in an entire food web, culminating in the largest creatures of all: the great whales. Tiny shrimp, known as krill, and small fish that feed on plankton are in turn preyed on by larger fish, which may be eaten by still larger fish or even whales. However, some of the largest whales feed directly on the plankton by swimming slowly through the surface layers, filtering the water to obtain enough of the tiny creatures to sustain them.

The most productive areas for plankton are places where cold currents well up from the ocean depths, carrying nutrients from the seabed to the surface sunlight. Here, billions of tiny creatures flourish and sustain small creatures that become food for seabirds, seals, and whales. Filter-feeding mollusks that thrive on plankton are dietary staples for such sea mammals as the walrus.

Several drifting creatures utilize winds blowing across the ocean's surface. The deadly Portuguese man-of-war has an air-filled sail that extends above the surface to catch air currents. As its long stinging tentacles stream out below in the water, its sail catches the wind and moves the animal over great distances, catching tiny organisms as it travels.

In the Depths

Light penetrates only a short distance below the ocean's surface. At moderate depths, where some light filters through, countless species of large open-ocean fish swim, some in shoals, some alone. They are streamlined and swift; with no place to hide, they must

The giant jellyfish, measuring up to 8 feet (2.5 meters) in length, drifts slowly and silently through deep water, ensnaring small fish and other creatures in its trailing tentacles.

both pursue their prey and avoid being captured themselves.

Large jellyfish, some as great as 8 feet (2.5 meters) across, drift in currents trailing deadly tentacles that extend downward 200 feet (61 meters). The giant squid, moving through water by jet propulsion, uses its ten arms to seize prey. With arms up to 30 feet (9.25 meters) long and a body as much as 18 feet (5.5 meters) in diameter, the giant squid is a true sea monster.

Into this underwater world come some of the air-breathing whales, sharks like the blue and porbeagle, and the enormous ocean sunfish, all in search of squid or fish.

The Seabed

Only in shallow seas and very clear water does any light reach the seabed. The depths know all-encompassing darkness, broken only by the flashing light of phosphorescent plankton and bioluminescent fish.

The great wealth of life in the upper parts of the oceans produces a huge quantity of organic waste matter. The excreta of birds, mammals, and fish; the dead bodies of these creatures; and the spent remains of billions of microscopic creatures all eventually fall to the seabed in a constant "snowstorm" of tiny particles. When it reaches the seabed, the waste material adds to the dense accumulation of debris already present, making it a productive feeding place for scavenging organisms.

In relatively shallow seas and on continental shelf areas, the seabed is especially productive. The rich silt, like the plankton, is the basis of an important series of food chains

Coral reefs thrive in warm, shallow water where they are home to many life forms and are visited by others. Here, schools of fish swimming by a reef off Hawaii have attracted the notice of a pair of gray reef sharks. Fish like these are food for such large creatures as sharks and whales.

The giant squid, with arms up to 30 feet (9.25 meters) long, is the largest of all the invertebrate animals. It is found at moderate depths in the colder oceans, tends to hunt in packs, and is known as a ferocious fighter when attacked.

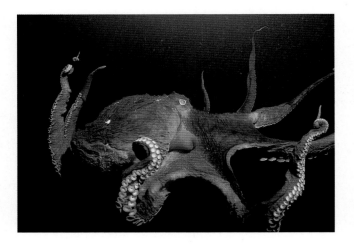

The repulsive appearance of the giant octopus, along with its arm spread of up to 12 feet (3.75 meters), has caused it to be known as a "devil fish." It is actually very shy and scurries away at the approach of humans.

forming a food web, with humans and the great whales as major predators. Seabed scavengers and filter-feeders feed directly on the organic matter and are preyed on by such creatures as crabs, squid, and larger fish, which in turn are taken by whales, other sea mammals, and humans.

Today's Oceans

The intricate web of life in the sea is endangered by the actions of humans. Overfishing and uncontrolled hunting have brought many species to the edge of extinction, while waste dumping in the ocean has increased pollution to dangerous levels. Any study of the giants of the sea and their behavior must be accompanied by an awareness that one day, because of humankind's behavior, many of them may vanish.

Following page: True giants of the sea, these breaching humpback whales provide a spectacle that must have struck awe and fear in early seagoing people.

THE CORAL REEF

Though individual coral animals are tiny, the colonies they produce and the reefs they form are quite large. Their growth has created atolls, lagoons, islands, and such coral complexes as Australia's Great Barrier Reef, which is 1,250 miles (2010 kilometers) long. In addition, coral reefs offer shelter and feeding grounds for many large, impressive creatures.

The warm, clear waters of the tropics provide perfect conditions for the growth of coral and the formation of a remarkable natural phenomenon, the coral reef. Countless millions of tiny organisms, both plants and animals, form one of the most intricate ecosystems in the world, creating the basis for a community of incredible variety and stunning beauty. The reef-building corals—soft-bodied animals encased in chalky skeletons—furnish the structure of the reef, which is then colonized by a vast array of plants, crustaceans, starfish, mollusks, and fish, each startling and colorful and perfectly adapted to life in this complex environment.

Reef Building

A coral is a small invertebrate animal that begins life as a tiny free-swimming larva, part of the plankton floating in the ocean currents. If the tiny larva survives the many plankton feeders in the ocean, it will settle on a suitable hard surface, preferably in a warm, shallow place with plenty of sunlight. Once settled, the larva grows into a tiny polyp with a mouth surrounded by tentacles. It secretes a hard external skeleton around itself, consisting mainly of calcium carbonate, or chalk.

Distinguished by brilliant color, the largest of the sea anemones live in tropical waters, where they gather planktonic animals for food with the stinging tentacles atop their bodies. But the brightly colored anemonefish that live in the protection of these tentacles are immune to the anemone's poison.

Instead of increasing its size by growth, a polyp divides to form two new polyps. This is a form of asexual reproduction that enables the numbers of individuals to increase. Each tiny polyp has its own skeleton, and these combine to form the basis of the reef. The individual polyps feed separately but are part of the same colony. Eventually the original polyps die, but their skeletons remain. As more and more individuals are formed by the division of existing corals, the colony increases in size, growing upward and outward, on the firm base provided by the original colonizers.

Several hundred species of coral have been identified in the world's reefs. Some are widespread and abundant, while others are more

The day octopus, measuring 5 feet (1.5 meters) in diameter, lives in crevices along the reefs of the Pacific. Like others of its kind, it is a complex mollusk with no shell at all. Its baglike body is very flexible, and its eight tentacles, capable of rapid movements, are joined at the base of the head by a web of skin.

rare and specialized, but all are built on the same basic plan.

Corals must live in shallow seas because their tissues contain millions of microscopic plants that require light in order to produce their food by photosynthesis. Even the clearest tropical water absorbs some of the light that passes through it, so that below a depth of about 165 feet (50 meters) there is not enough light energy to be useful to plants. Corals cannot tolerate exposure to the air, so the upper limit of their colonization is the lowest point to which the tides fall—the extreme low-water mark of spring tides. No coral polyp can survive in a free-floating state, since it must be anchored in order to build its chalky skeleton. These three restrictions limit the corals to warm, clear, relatively shallow waters with an abundance of firm rocks.

Each reef contains many species of coral, and in some particularly rich reefs over two hundred different species have been identified. Some of these are the important reef builders, which are long-lived and form solid structures, while others are colonizers, able to live on the reef as long as they receive some support and protection from other corals. Some corals are very delicate and grow only in sheltered places, while others prefer exposed sites. Corals appear to grow best on the edge of the reef, particularly on the seaward side, where they receive some exposure to wave action; this keeps them supplied with food in the form of plankton and plenty of oxygen for respiration. Waste products are also carried away easily.

The following examples are but a cross-section of the many disparate life forms found on coral reefs. Other reef creatures (discussed later) include some sharks, groupers, and other large fish.

Reef sharks find most of their food close to the reef and spend much of their time cruising along near the bottom or along submerged cliff edges.

The tentacles of the orange cup coral polyps show the many stinging cells used to immobilize prey. This particular specimen was photographed at night on a shipwreck in the British Virgin Islands.

Sponges are simple, primitive, filter-feeding animals. The largest grows up to 9 feet (2.75 meters) in height, so sizable that a human can stand inside them.

Sponges

In addition to the great variety of corals, a host of other animals lives on reefs. Many, like sponges, are filter feeders, drawing in a constant stream of sea water. These are among the most primitive of animals, but they can develop quite large colonies in favorable conditions. Some become quite large, measuring up to 9 feet (2.75 meters) long. The porous surface of a sponge is made up of thousands of tiny holes through which water is sucked in by special feeding cells. All the pores ultimately connect to a larger opening, which expels filtered water along with any waste products.

Some sponges are brilliantly colored, adding to the overall attractiveness of the reefs. The color is usually due to the presence of microscopic plants living inside the sponge tissues—the same arrangement that occurs in many corals. This partnership between a simple animal and a simple plant, beneficial to both, is known as symbiosis. The phenomenon is surprisingly widespread in the living world, especially in complex environments such as coral reefs.

Eels

Perhaps the most feared eel is the vicious moray. Their average maximum length is 5 feet (1.5 meters), but some occasionally grow to 10 feet (3 meters). Armed with sharp teeth and an acute sense of smell, the moray hides in reef crevices, remaining out of sight until unsuspecting prey is close enough to be seized with a rapid outward lunge and a powerful snap of the jaws. Because of this lightning-attack strategy, the moray is considered a dangerously aggressive species.

Unlike free-swimming fish, which breathe by opening their mouths as they swim, the stationary moray must gulp water constantly to get enough oxygen. Since there must always be water flowing over their gills, they gulp down food very quickly, thus giving rise to their reputation as fierce predators.

A green moray eel slides from its hiding place at the base of a reef in the Bahamas. Though shy of humans, it will attack people with ferocity if it feels itself trapped or threatened.

The viper eel, its vicious teeth bared, hides in coral crevices, waiting to gulp down passing prey. However, its mouth is not as ravenous as it seems. The fish must continually draw in water over the gills to get enough oxygen to breathe.

are actually part of their bodies. Beneath the arms are rows of tube feet—suckerlike structures filled with water—which can be extended and retracted to pull the animal along. The tube feet can exert a strong grip, enabling the starfish to pull on the two halves of a small mollusk's shell and wrench them apart to feed on the contents.

At a maximum of 3 feet (.9 meter) across, the largest starfish species are hardly huge, but they appear so when compared to their much smaller kin, which sometimes measure as small as 1/2 inch (1.25 centimeters) in diameter. It can be startling for human divers to come across these yard-wide star-shaped creatures.

In spite of this reputation, they attack humans only when strongly provoked. Exploring a reef at night could be dangerous if morays are out feeding and one of them is inadvertently made to feel cornered by human movements. There is added danger when morays are caught by humans for food. About five species are violently poisonous, causing death in one-tenth of reported cases.

Starfish

Starfish—or sea stars—are spiny-skinned animals related to sea urchins and sea cucumbers. They feed on mollusks and sometimes live by scavenging. Common on some reefs, they have five arms, which are not appendages but

Giant Clams

One of the largest denizens of the reef, and imposing by any standards, is the giant clam. As with many other reef dwellers, this huge mollusk lives by filter feeding. The clam opens its enormous shell and draws water in through a feeding siphon. Inside the hard shell is the living tissue. The visible part, known as the mantle, is often brightly colored, once again due to the presence of millions of microscopic plants. Giant clams thrive in sunny places, as the microscopic plants, or algae, in their tissues require light energy to grow and multiply. As the algae increase, they are absorbed into the clam's body as food.

Embedded in the mantle are light-sensitive eye spots. If a shadow falls across the clam, indicating a possible threat, it can respond quickly by closing up its shell. When the two halves of the shell snap together, the force is strong enough to break a human leg. Divers are well advised not to tempt their luck and get inside a clam. There are tales of people walking over a reef at low tide and inadvertently stepping into the open shell of a clam partly concealed in the coral. In such cases the valves close up, trapping the unfortunate person.

THE GREAT WHALES

The largest living creatures ever known on earth are the great whales. Though the dinosaurs have come and gone, none of them ever rivaled the blue whale in size. At over 100 feet (30.5 meters) in length, a full-grown blue whale is a giant by any reckoning. Furthermore, apart from the higher primates and the elephants, these immense mammals are the most intelligent of animals.

Whales, along with dolphins, belong to the order Cetacea; this group is further divided into two suborders. The first, the Mysticeti, includes the baleen whales, such as the blue, fin, and humpback. In the second, the Orthodoceti, are found the toothed whales, including the sperm whale and the most notorious of all, the killer whale, which despite its name is also the largest of the dolphins.

Baleen Whales

Baleen whales range in size from the blue whale at up to 100 feet (30.5 meters) long to the minke whale measuring just over 29 feet (9 meters). Whales in this group have no teeth; instead they have a large comblike structure called baleen, which hangs down in plates from the roof of the mouth to filter sea water and trap food. There are two blowholes in the top of the head for breathing.

The characteristics of the baleen plates vary from species to species. The plankton feeders, for example, have very fine baleen, while that of blue whales is slightly coarse, allowing them to trap krill, an abundant species of shrimp measuring just under 1/2 inch (1 centimeter) in length. A number of baleen whales, such as the minke and humpback, are primarily fish eaters, so their baleen is shorter and stronger than that of plankton feeders. Gray whales, feeding mainly on mollusks and crustaceans dredged out of the mud in shallow seas, have the coarsest baleen of all.

This humpback whale uses a technique called lunge feeding to catch herring and krill. It then settles into the water, closes its mouth, and strains the water through its baleen plates, trapping thousands of fish.

The body of the gray whale is dark gray with lighter, mottled patches. It always has a heavy encrustation of barnacles and whale lice on its skin, especially around the head.

The right whales—so-called because they were the "right" whales to hunt—feed on microscopic plants and animals. They are bulky, round-headed creatures with huge heads and mouths, occupying about one-third of the body. In fact, the mouth is so large that it would be possible for a dozen people to stand inside it. The upper jaw is long and narrow, with an arched shape to help support the baleen plates. Right whales feed in waters close to shore and are slow swimmers, thus making them easy targets for early whalers in small boats. Once harpooned and killed, they yielded a rich store of blubber, whale meat, and "whale bone," as baleen was then called.

The gray whale is slenderer than the right whale, and its head is far less bulky; the upper jaw is arched and narrow. Its body is a distinct mottled gray and is usually encrusted with patches of whale lice and barnacles. At one time it was known as "devil fish" because of its vigorous defense when attacked by early whalers. Today, when confronted by an unthreatening boat full of whale watchers, it will approach gently and allow itself to be touched.

Rorquals

Included among the baleen whales are the rorquals, the family boasting the largest of all living things, the blue whale. All rorquals are streamlined, fast swimmers. Their jaw line is fairly straight, and below it are many throat grooves which allow the mouth and throat to expand enormously when feeding. Inside the mouth, the baleen plates are fairly short.

The baleen of right whales, like that of other plankton feeders, is extremely fine, allowing it to trap quantities of microscopic plants and animals.

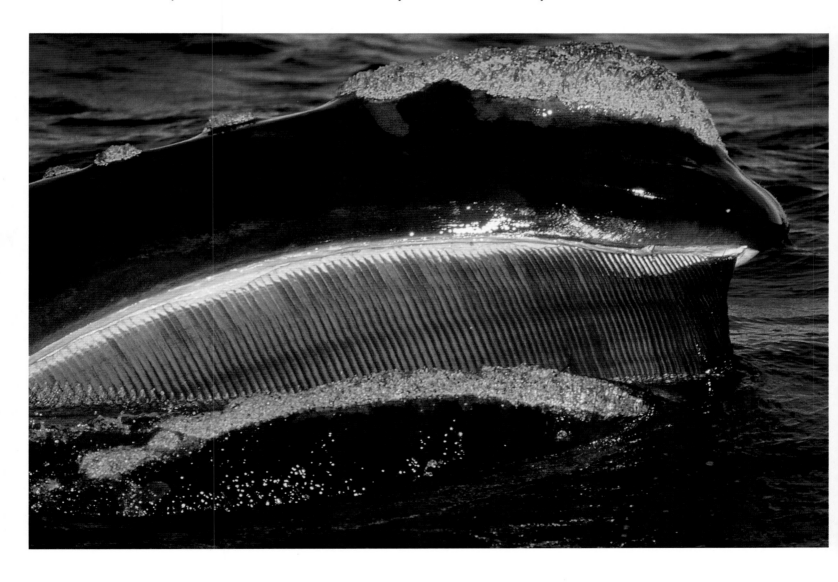

When the whale begins a deep dive its head is pointed downward, and the tail comes up and out above the surface before finally disappearing, leaving only a swirl in the water.

Whale lice insert their strong legs into the skin of the whale and create indentations in which they live and feed. Other whale parasites are diatoms, microscopic plant forms that create shells around themselves.

Following page: Humpback whales often cooperate to feed on a large shoal of fish, driving it into a tight formation before breaking through the surface together with their mouths open.

The largest animal of all, the blue whale, is seen for the giant it is in this aerial photograph. It has returned to the surface to breathe by emptying its lungs with a loud, rushing sound and a column of water called a blow.

Like its giant cousin the blue whale, the fin whale is a rorqual. It is slightly smaller than the blue—90 feet (27.5 meters) long—and has a reputation as a fighter. There are recorded instances of hunted fin whales that turned to ram and sink pursuing whaling ships.

Typical of rorquals, this humpback is feeding with its throat grooves expanded, allowing it to take into its mouth a huge volume of food-filled water.

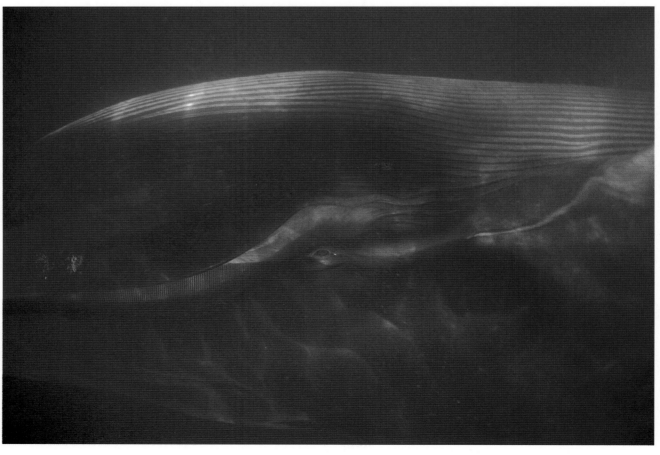

Five of the rorquals are rather similar in appearance, differing only in size. The largest is the blue whale, followed by the fin, sei, tropical (Bryde's), and minke. The humpback is also a rorqual, but it is not a sleek animal. It is far more bulky than the others, with extremely long, white flippers, a strange, knobby head, and fewer throat grooves. More active at the surface than other rorquals, it is frequently found near the shore.

Toothed Whales

The toothed whales range in size from the sperm whale, at up to 60 feet (18.5 meters) long, to other giants like the killer whale and some beaked whales, at 35 feet (10.5 meters) long, down to the most familiar, dolphins, at 6 feet (1.85 meters) long. Their food consists mainly of fish, squid, crustaceans, and in some cases, other marine mammals. Each species shows a special adaptation to its method of feeding or type of food. Many of the smaller species feed in shallow waters close to shore,

while others live in the open ocean, far from land. Toothed whales have a single blowhole on the top of the head for breathing.

The sperm whale, the largest toothed whale, has special qualities that have made it legendary. Everything about this whale is extraordinary: its great size and immense head; its ability to dive over 3,000 feet (915 meters) and stay down for over an hour; its ferocity when hunted; and its body, packed with oils and other valuable commodities. Though hunting the sperm whale was always dangerous, thousands were taken each year during the whaling boom. Today, with stocks depleted, this species is harder to find.

The sperm whale hunts its food in total darkness, far below the ocean's surface, and finds it by a form of echo-location. It is thought to be able to produce high-frequency sounds that are strong enough to stun prey. Its favorite food is the giant squid, which with arms 30 feet (9.25 meters) long is a formidable opponent. The fierce battles between these two ani-

The deep-diving sperm whale lowers its huge head to begin a dive. Once below the surface it may not appear for an hour, but often comes up close to the spot from which it dived.

A spy-hopping whale sticks its head vertically out of the water until the eye is exposed and then slips back down again without a splash. This killer whale may be behaving in this way to view surrounding waters or other animals.

The killer whale is a highly successful predator. Not only is it equipped with sharp teeth and powerful jaws, but its sleek body makes it fast. It can even move at great speed across the surface of the water to capture prey.

A killer whales lunges powerfully onto the beach, where it will snatch up a sea lion pup from the edge of the surf.

mals often result in circular scars along the whale's flank and around its head.

The enlarged, bulbous head of the sperm whale is made up mostly of an oily substance called spermaceti. This material can solidify at low temperatures and is thought to help alter the buoyancy of the whale and assist it in diving and ascending.

The streamlined killer whale is recognized by its black-and-white markings, and, in the case of males, a dorsal fin reaching 6.5 feet (2-meters). Killer whales are actually classified as dolphins. Supreme ocean hunters, they run in groups varying from three or four to as many as forty individuals and are the equivalent of wolf packs on land. Some are wide ranging, hunting over a vast ocean area. Others are more restricted, preferring to stay in one area, such as a large bay, where they can exploit all the food sources available.

The killer whale's impressive array of teeth enables it to catch and kill anything from fish and birds to large sharks and seals. It will even prey on other whales. Packs of killer whales have been known to attack the enormous blue whale, tearing chunks from its body and worrying it until it dies of blood loss and exhaustion. Many killer whales position themselves near strong currents in river mouths, where they capture large fish like salmon. Some even ride the surf onto a beach and pluck seals from their resting place at the water's edge, while others attack seals on polar ice floes.

Fond of deep water, beaked whales are so rarely seen that little is known about them. They have bulbous heads and a long, tapering snout that gives them their name. With only one or two pairs of teeth, they are able to catch squid, their principal food.

The unusual beluga whale is all white. Its body, lacking a dorsal fin, is attached by a flexible neck to its bulbous head. The average length of an adult male is 16 feet (4.85 meters). Belugas winter in the Arctic regions, where they feed on fish and live in groups of ten to twenty adults. However, they often come together in large schools of several hundred when migrating to northern rivers, where they spend the summer. They are particularly known for the curious trilling calls they make while hunting.

Aside from their color, beluga whales are noted for their expressive faces and flexible necks. When they gather in schools to feed, their chirping and squealing sounds can sometimes be heard on the shore.

Appearance and Habits

Due to their hydrodynamic shape, most whales are very fast swimmers. With their elongated bodies, covered with smooth, hairless skin, they can achieve great speeds with little water resistance. The slower-moving species, such as the right and the bowhead, are fairly rotund in shape but are designed for quick turning in shallow waters.

The whale's tail lies horizontally in the water and is attached to its body by a muscular tail stock that provides power for swimming. Forward movement comes mostly from the upstroke of the tail, the downstroke being a more relaxed movement. Steering and balance are maintained by the flippers and movements of the body. To begin a dive, a whale lowers its head and gives a powerful stroke of the tail, which propels the entire body downward.

In some species, most notably the humpback, the back is arched prominently when diving and the tail rises out of the water. As the

A breaching humpback whale is a thrilling sight. This exciting behavior, which is sometimes repeated many times, may be a form of communication or a play activity in young males.

A female whale gives birth to a single calf and may suckle it for up to ten months. As a result of the close bond between parent and offspring, the calf never strays very far from its mother and stays close for protection for an extended period.

Humpback whales have black-and-white markings beneath their tails, which are unique to each whale, enabling them to be recognized individually.

Like some of their larger kin, the great whales, dolphins enjoy their own form of breaching. The circular pattern of water drops around this spinner dolphin is a stop-action illustration of how the animal rotates its body as it leaps completely clear of the water and propels itself forward a considerable distance.

In classic form, a trio of common dolphins races ahead of a moving boat in an arcing line of sequential dives. This behavior is known as bowheading.

body continues to slip below the surface, the tail gives a further upstroke, leaving a circular, oily-looking swirl on the surface called a fluke print.

A number of whale species indulge in a spectacular behavior known as breaching, in which the whale leaps out of the water and falls back with a huge splash. Young humpback whales regularly engage in breaching, sometimes completely leaving the water. Other breaching whales include the right, killer, and sperm whales.

For an animal like the humpback whale, weighing many tons, leaping clear of the water must require a huge amount of energy and strength. It has been estimated that only two or three powerful beats of the tail are required to get the whale out of the water.

Dolphins and porpoises, the smaller members of the whale family, are well known for their own form of breaching. Many enjoy bow-riding, a series of repeated leaps forward in front of a moving vessel. This is a habit they acquired by swimming in front of large whales. Perhaps the most spectacular feat is performed by the spinner dolphin, which rotates swiftly on the axis of its body as it leaps from the water in a forward-moving path.

In spite of their names, pilot whales are large, sociable dolphins, reaching up to 20 feet (6 meters) in length. Unlike the loner shown here, they often live in large schools, feeding on deep sea fish and squid.

SEA MAMMALS

Besides whales and dolphins, there are other sea mammals—such as walruses, seals, and sea lions—that are not so fully evolved that they can spend their entire lives in the water. They must come onto land or ice to give birth, and while some species are at sea for extended periods, others spend time ashore each day, resting between spells of feeding.

Walruses
The walrus is a massive, seal-like mammal with a bristling mustache and a pair of long tusks. The enormous, hairless body, usually reddish in color and sometimes reaching a length of 12 feet (3.75 meters), is ungainly on land, but graceful and fast moving in water.

This gregarious, highly social animal is almost always found in large concentrations. Walruses generally cluster on ice floes or stony shores. As the polar ice advances and retreats, they migrate in large herds, and only rarely does one individual become lost and find itself south of its Arctic home, perhaps reaching the shores of northern Britain.

Raking the seabed with their nearly 3 1/2-foot- (1-meter-) long tusks, walruses unearth cockles, clams, and other buried mollusks. They locate this food by using the sensory bristles around the mouth. To a lesser extent, walruses also feed on fish and sometimes smaller seals. Occasionally a tusk is damaged, perhaps by hitting a buried rock, but the walrus can still feed. Apparently healthy individuals are frequently seen with one tusk much shorter than the other.

The huge tusks of the walrus sometimes reach almost 3 1/2 feet (I meter) in length and are used to gouge through the mud on the seabed to dig out clams. At first juveniles have short tusks, but soon after weaning, they begin to grow.

Northern islands are favorite hauling-out sites for walruses, highly social animals that enjoy each other's company. Hundreds can be counted at times, covering entire beaches.

Sirenians

The sirenians, or sea cows, are a group of water-dwelling mammals that includes the dugong and manatee. Reaching a length of 13 feet (3.9 meters) and weighing up to 1,100 pounds (498 kilograms), they are distantly related to elephants and look like grossly overweight, lethargic dolphins. Unlike seals and walruses, they are completely aquatic and cannot leave the water and move about on land. They inhabit warm, shallow seas and are fond of estuaries and sluggish rivers, where they feed on sea grasses and other succulent aquatic vegetation. Sirenians have virtually no body hair, except bristles around the mouth, and are covered with loose, leathery skin. The head is large, merging into the bulky body without any sign of a neck.

Sirenians are reported to suckle their young by resting upright in the water and supporting the pup gently with one flipper. This tender scene is thought to be the origin of the mermaid legend.

This dugong is feeding on sea grass in a shallow bay in the Indian Ocean. Unlike the manatee, it has a distinct neck and a two-fluked, whale-shaped tail.

The 13-foot (3.9-meter) manatee is actually a gentle giant. Shy of humans, it usually swims off at the sound of a boat. A few have learned to trust swimmers and may allow themselves to be touched.

Seals

Seals are earless animals with sleek bodies and paddlelike flippers, which are not very effective for land movement. In the water, however, seals move swiftly, using their smooth, muscular bodies to great advantage in swimming after prey or in escaping predators.

Among the larger seals, the gray seal reaches a length of 10 feet (3 meters) and a weight of 616 pounds (279 kilograms). The species prefers rocky, exposed places in remote coastal areas and is found mostly around the shores of Britain. This deep-diving animal reaches depths of at least 330 feet (100 meters) in search of large fish. The bull gray seal can be recognized by its "Roman" nose and great bulk. It often bears scars from battles with other bulls during mating season. Another deep-diving seal, the bearded seal is also very large. Its extra-long whiskers are highly sensitive and help the seal find food, mostly mollusks and crustaceans, on the seabed.

Antarctic Seals

The Antarctic is home to three other seal species. The most abundant of these is the crabeater seal, which actually eats krill rather than crab, and measures up to 10 feet (3 meters) in length. It is confined to the ever-shifting pack ice and does not form large colonies, but lives in scattered groups of twos and threes. The crabeater's enemy is the killer whale, which hunts it among the ice floes.

Leopard seals are noted for their ferocity. They prey on penguins, large fish, and the young of other seals. These seals have a natural cunning, enabling them to cooperate and collectively terrorize penguin colonies during the breeding season. In such situations, two seals position themselves near a colony and ambush penguins returning from fishing trips. With a deft flick of the head, the seal can skin and eat a penguin in a few seconds.

Weddell seals are commonly found on the coastal Antarctic ice. They are deep divers able to stay down for long periods, reaching depths of over 1,980 feet (604 meters) in dives lasting over an hour. From the surface it is sometimes possible to hear the twittering, birdlike calls they use to locate fish in the dark.

A leopard seal chases a hapless Adelie penguin across ice-filled water. These Antarctic birds, which form large colonies to breed, are an abundant food source for this seal species.

Following page: Weddell seals inhabit the coastal ice floes of Antarctica. They enjoy basking in the sun and sleep soundly in the open for long periods. In winter they remain in the water all the time, keeping breathing holes open in the ice by gnawing through with their teeth.

Elephant Seals

Elephant seals are the real giants among seals. With adult males reaching a length of 21 1/2 feet (6.5 meters), no other sea mammals rival them apart from the great whales. The elephant seals are divided into two species, the northern and southern.

The southern elephant seal—the more abundant—inhabits many sub-Antarctic areas in the southern oceans. This seal spends much of the winter at sea, often at considerable distances from land, feeding on fish and squid caught by deep diving. In spring, some haul out on ice floes, but most prefer beaches. Mature males are the first to arrive, and claim beach areas with aggressive displays. In such displays, the animal inflates its bulbous nose, or trunk, increasing the apparent size of the head and helping to intensify the loudness and resonance of its roar. If one male approaches another's territory too closely, a fierce battle ensues until one of them gives up and moves away.

After the males have established territories the pregnant females arrive. The males organize them into groups, and the young are born within a week. The pups grow rapidly and are weaned within a few weeks. During this time, the mothers mate and are ready to return to the sea. Together with the males, the pups—which by now have developed sleek coats—also start to leave the beaches, and soon the scene of all this frenzied activity is deserted.

Food reserves are replenished in midsummer as the seals feed ravenously. They then return to the beach, where they molt off their worn coats and grow new fur. After this, the seals return again to the sea to fatten up during the winter.

Sea Lions

Sea lions are thought to have first appeared in the northern Pacific Ocean. They later spread out to colonize areas in the Southern Hemisphere. Though resembling seals, they are distinguished from them by the presence of ear flaps.

The best-known of these is the California sea lion, which when used as a performing animal is called a "trained seal." Much larger is the Steller's sea lion, which reaches 11 feet (3.5 meters) long and is the most northerly in its range, favoring the Aleutian Islands.

At the other end of the world is the Australian sea lion, which is very large, growing to 14 feet (4.25 meters) in length. It is a striking animal with a thick coat and massive shoulders. To match their large bulk, they have an aggressive disposition and seem to be continually battling each other, even out of mating season.

Steller's sea lions compete with fishermen and are hunted in some parts of their range, so they are wary if approached by a boat. They often haul out in places such as this, which allow them a rapid escape into deep water if danger threatens.

The elephant seal, the largest seal species in the world, probably earned its name from the grotesquely enlarged proboscis, used by bulls as part of a threat display in arguments over territory.

Two large bull elephant seals square up to each other. Much time is spent in dispute over the ownership of prime stretches of beach, and arguments sometimes end in bloodshed.

SHARKS AND RAYS

For centuries sharks have been thought of as fearless killers and a danger to humans. The sight of the pointed snout, the large mouth, the cold, unblinking eyes, the triangular fins, and the sinuous body is enough to cause terror in most people.

Out of three hundred shark species, only twenty-seven have been known to attack humans or their boats. Shark attacks are well publicized, but statistics show that there is little likelihood of a swimmer being attacked unless very close to a member of a dangerous species.

Sharks

Sharks are primitive fish with a skeleton composed of cartilage rather than bone. Unlike true fish, they have a covering of rough, back-

Manta rays are the largest of all rays, with a "wingspan" of up to 23 feet (7 meters). Although this is an enormous fish, it feeds only on the tiniest creatures, taking very small shrimp in addition to plankton.

The gaping mouth of the great white shark shows the frightening array of teeth that it uses to tear chunks of flesh from its prey. It readily attacks any marine mammal or large fish, and human divers must take extreme care if great whites are in the vicinity.

Blue sharks are beautifully stream-lined, fast-swim-ming denizens of the open ocean. They are voracious predators that feed mainly at night. Here, though, a blue shark makes a daylight attack on a school of anchovies.

The huge megamouth shark is a recently discovered species and is very rarely seen alive. It inhabits deep water, where it feeds on plankton and tiny shrimp. It has special light-emitting cells around its mouth.

An oceanic whitetip shark, its fearsome fin cutting through the water, swims along near the sur-face in search of prey. This is one of the most common sharks of the open ocean and grows to a length of 16 feet (4.85 meters).

ward-pointing, toothlike scales, and gill slits instead of gill flaps.

In most species, the teeth are triangular with either a smooth or serrated edge. The larger species have such a capacious mouth that they can swallow an extraordinary variety of objects: bottles, ship's tackle, human clothing, and such land animals as reindeer. Most of the time, however, they confine their feeding to the prey to which they are most suited. Sharks are mostly fish eaters, but will take other food such as marine mammals, seabirds, and turtles.

A shark's senses are designed to help it locate food in the sea. The eyes can detect movement in quite dim light, and are focused in such a way that distant objects can be seen clearly, giving the shark warning of approaching prey or danger.

The shark's most important sense is smell. Most sharks are able to locate prey by scent alone, having the ability to detect tiny quantities of blood or body fluid in the water. With its nostrils placed on either side of the head, the shark turns its head from side to side as it swims, to determine the direction from which the scent of prey is coming. It then swims toward the scent in decreasing circles until finally homing in on it, often using the eyes at the last moment to guide a precise attack.

A mackerel makes a tasty snack for a hungry blue shark and comprises one of the principal parts of its diet.

Fierce Predators

The tiger shark, which reaches 20 feet (6 meters) in length, has a reputation for eating anything that fits in its mouth, including car tires and human beings. It is, therefore, one of the most dangerous sharks ever encountered. Another aggressive shark, the hammerhead,

Almost as fierce and feared as the great white, the notorious tiger shark is noted for its attacks on humans. A 14 foot (4.25 meter) tiger shark usually weighs around 1,400 pounds (635 kilograms).

A tiger shark feeds on the carcass of a sperm whale. This species will eat anything it finds, including mammals, birds, fish, lobsters, crabs, and even tin cans. It is particularly fond of sea turtles and will pursue and take them if possible.

Scalloped hammerheads, like those in this school swimming off the Galapagos Islands, typically spend time hunting fish near the surface. However, they can also descend to great depths in order to catch fish near the seabed, locating prey in the dark by using their ability to detect electrical currents.

The scalloped hammerhead has a sleek and smooth body shape like most other sharks and is a fast swimmer. However, its strange head is unique; the eyes are located at the ends of the scalloped head projections.

Swimming across an Australian coral reef, a tiger shark calmly swallows a passing fish. Like its equally predatory namesake on land, this shark is marked with a bold pattern of stripes along its sides.

has also been known to attack humans. It measures 16 1/2 feet (5 meters) long and has bizarre protuberances on either side of its head that support the eyes.

The shark feared most by humans is the great white. Though its average length is around 16 1/2 feet (5 meters), exceptional individuals measuring 36 feet (11 meters) have been recorded. However large, the great white is unpredictable and should be treated with respect. This species, often called the man-eater, accounts for most verified attacks on humans.

Shark Attack

The reasons for shark attacks on humans are not clear. They could be caused by sheer aggression, self-defense, or hunger. One important factor is water temperature. At

A face-to-face confrontation between a great white and two divers in a shark cage. This sea giant has been lured with fish bait so the divers can photograph it at close range. The feared great white shark is one of the largest and most dangerous predators in the ocean.

Moving relentlessly upward with its mouth open, a great white shark is apparently swimming toward unsuspecting prey, which it has detected with its keen senses.

The rows of triangular teeth in the mouth of this great white shark are continually being replaced; as the front teeth wear out, new teeth are ready to grow in from behind. Each tooth has a serrated edge to give it greater cutting power.

Cloudy seas are usually rich in plankton, the food of the basking shark. It can be found in the Pacific and off the coasts of Europe, where it frequents shallow waters.

The whale shark is a gentle giant that can reach a length of 66 feet (20 meters). Although formidable in size and appearance, it feeds on nothing more than plankton, cruising slowly near the surface, drawing water into its huge mouth, and filtering out tiny organisms.

around 70 degrees F (21 degrees C) shark aggression increases dramatically. The shark's acute senses certainly play a role. Since sharks are attracted to blood in the water, spear-fishermen who carry their catch around with them are especially at risk. Swimmers making splashy movements in clear, calm water are more vulnerable than bathers in shallow surf with wave action. However, those diving into deeper water from a boat, especially if people are fishing from it, are in greater peril. And divers who take liberties with sharks, approaching too closely to photograph them or even tweaking their tails, should not be surprised if they are attacked.

The Filter Feeders

Not all sharks are carnivorous; some are plankton feeders. They take only the smallest organisms by filter feeding. Some of these are also the largest fish in the sea. Basking sharks are usually 23 feet (7 meters) long, while some have measured 43 feet (13 meters). They feed by cruising along slowly near the surface, where plankton is most plentiful, and taking in sea water with their vast gaping mouths. Water is strained through their sievelike gill rakers, and the plankton is trapped and swallowed.

A similar species is the whale shark, which is even larger. Its average length is 35 feet (10.5 meters), but some individuals grow to 60 feet (18.5 meters). Whale sharks are not only long, but they are massive in proportion, having unbelievably large mouths and very bulky bodies.

Rays

Rays are similar to sharks in some ways, having cartilaginous skeletons, rough skin, and gill slits. Their bodies are flattened from top to bottom—unlike true flatfish, such as the

Following page: A manta ray feeding on plankton. "Horns" on either side of the head help direct food into the mouth. Once feared by humans, the manta ray is actually toothless and is unable to eat any large creatures at all.

This stingray has covered itself with sand by rippling its wings, so it can lie still on the bottom and blend in perfectly with the seabed.

halibut, which are flattened laterally and swim on their sides.

Like sharks, rays have various feeding methods. Some are active predators, some scavengers, and some plankton feeders. The flattened body is an adaptation to life on the seabed and helps the fish to hide from predators or remain concealed until prey approaches closely. However, some rays are free swimming and can be seen near the surface of the open sea.

With striking black-and-white markings, the magnificent manta ray is a huge plankton feeder. It may measure up to 22 feet (6.75 meters) wide and weigh as much as 3,000 pounds (1,357 kilograms). It cruises along just below the surface, with the tips of its "wings" just breaking the waves from time to time. Feeding fins on either side of the front of the head help sweep plankton into the mouth.

Sometimes manta rays breach, leaping clear of the water. It was once feared as a "black devil," but aside from the risk of its great bulk causing a small vessel to capsize, it poses little threat to humans. This is a widespread species generally found in the warmer waters of the world's oceans.

Stingrays produce an electric shock from special cells located on their tails. They use this to defend against predators rather than as a means to kill prey, which is easily seized with the mouth. If a stingray is picked up by the tail, the resulting shock can be quite startling. In common with most other species, stingrays have excellent camouflage and can conceal themselves on the ocean bottom by lying still. They often improve their camouflage by rippling the wings as they settle, stirring up bottom sediment that lands on their backs, causing them to look even more like the seabed.

A southern stingray swims slowly over the seabed showing its "wings," which enable it to make graceful, gliding movements. Its mouth is hidden on the underside of its head.

Stingrays are most abundant in warm coastal seas and are often found in quite shallow water. This southern stingray is hovering over a coral reef in the Bahamas. Like other stingrays, it bears a venomous spine near the base of its tail.

GIANT FISH AND TURTLES

The deep ocean is home to two types of sea creatures that can grow to imposing size: the bony fish and the marine turtles. Bony fish, characterized by a bony skeleton, gill flaps over the gills, and disklike scales on the body, range in size from tiny to quite large, both in length and weight. Because of their size, the largest species of this group continually challenges both commercial and sport fishermen.

Tuna
The largest bony fish are the tuna, and the largest of these is the bluefin, known as the "titan of tuna." It grows to a length of 14 feet (4.25 meters) and a weight of 1,800 pounds (814 kilograms). With their long, smooth, muscular bodies, and fins that retract into grooves to reduce drag, tuna are extremely fast swimmers. Their blood system is designed so

Groupers are large, bony fish that live among rocks and in crevices, often near coral reefs. This particular individual, a member of the species known as the potato cod, is seen at a point on the Great Barrier Reef known as the Cod Hole.

This school of bluefin tuna shows clearly how well adapted these sleek fish are to swimming at high speed over great distances. They are voracious carnivores and eat large quantities of smaller fish like mackerel.

Wrasses range in size from tiny, pencil-like species to the giant humpback wrasse, which measures up to 10 feet (3 meters) long. The giants favor tropical reefs and temperate marine waters.

that tissues conserve heat, making the fish's body warmer than the surrounding water, thus enabling its muscles to work efficiently.

Ocean Sunfish

The heaviest bony fish is the bizarre ocean sunfish. From head to tail the average sunfish is 6.5 feet (2 meters), while from the tip of the dorsal fin to the tip of the anal fin it measures 8 feet (2.5 meters). Though not as long as the tuna or some sharks, the sunfish is bulky and rotund and may weigh over 1 ton (.9 metric tons).

The sunfish earned its name from its apparent habit of basking in the warm sunlight near the ocean surface. However, it is probable that sunfish that do this are either sick or under stress, since their real home is the deep sea, where they feed on smaller fish and squid.

One of the strangest of all fish, the ocean sunfish looks only half finished. It appears to be all head with no body or tail. Its tough skin has a thick layer of armor beneath it, providing protection from most creatures in the sea.

The marlin is a well-known sport fish with various species found in both the Atlantic and the Pacific. Perhaps the largest of the family is the black marlin with weights recorded up to 1,560 pounds (705 kilograms). The individual shown here is a blue marlin swimming in the waters off Hawaii.

The strong, fast-swimming Atlantic sailfish is noted for its tall, magnificent dorsal fin. Like other billfish, it uses the bill to attack and stun its victims as it swims through schools of mackerel or other food fish.

Marlin, Swordfish, and Sailfish

These billed creatures are large fish of the open ocean, long sought by fishermen who enjoy the spirited way they fight when hooked. All have a long, pointed upper jaw or bill, which may be used to stun smaller prey fish. Sometimes when caught by an angler, a swordfish's struggle is so great that its long bill, often one-third of its body length, is driven through the wooden hull of the fishing boat.

Both the marlin and swordfish can weigh as much as 1,000 pounds (305 kilograms) and reach lengths of 15 feet (4.5 meters). The 11-foot (3.5-meter) sailfish is distinguished by its greatly enlarged, bright blue dorsal fin. This fish is a sportsman's favorite because of the spectacular way it leaps out of the water when hooked.

Barracudas

Barracudas are smaller than fish like marlin, but still reach impressive lengths, growing as long as 6.5 feet (2 meters). What they lack in size, they make up for in formidable strength and fierce behavior. Fast swimmers with large jaws and sharp teeth, they can catch any fish they choose. In some areas, they are as feared as the much larger sharks. Sometimes called "monsters of the deep," they have been known to attack human swimmers. They appear to feed by sight rather than smell and are attracted to bright objects and erratic movements, explaining their interest in people swimming and splashing in the water.

The great barracuda may reach a length of over 10 feet (3 meters) and is a very strong fish. It feeds on a variety of smaller fish and is very fond of schooling fish like mackerel, which it consumes in huge quantities.

Groupers and Sea Basses

Groupers and sea basses, known to scientists as serranids, are large-mouthed fish found in tropical and temperate seas, some growing to a considerable size: 12 feet (3.75 meters) long and weighing 1,000 pounds (455 kilograms). There are nearly four hundred species in this family, ranging in size from very small to quite large. They exhibit a wide variety of colors and markings, but all have the same basic body plan and general appearance. The back is topped with two dorsal fins, the first of which is armed with sharp spines. A striking feature is the very thick lips of the large mouth, which aid in capturing and consuming prey. Almost all are carnivores and have been seen to take fish, crustaceans, squids, and octopuses. The larger species are fairly sluggish in their movements, never wandering far from their territories on a reef or shipwreck.

The giant sea bass weighs up to 800 pounds (362 kilograms) and is found off the California coast and in Caribbean waters, where it is sometimes sought after by sport fishermen. Its serranid cousin, the Nassau grouper, is particularly fascinating in its ability to change colors. This fish has eight distinct color phases ranging from dark brown to cream. The Queensland grouper is a common fish along Australia's Great Barrier Reef. Found also in many other parts of the Indo-Pacific, it is the largest known grouper, achieving a weight of up to 1,000 pounds (455 kilograms).

Marine Turtles

Marine turtles have beautifully curved shells and long flippers to ease movement through

Following page: Marine turtles, such as this loggerhead, must breathe air like all other reptiles. Though it can swim beneath the water for extended periods, it must return to the surface from time to time.

Marine turtles nest on beaches, usually coming ashore at night to avoid predators. The process of crawling up the beach, digging the nest, depositing the eggs, and returning to the sea is a lengthy one, taking many hours.

The enormous giant sea bass, sometimes weighing nearly 880 pounds (398 kilograms), has sandy markings that help it blend in with its surroundings. A fish of this size has few predators, but it is a slow swimmer and, if pursued, does not escape easily.

the sea. A swimming turtle appears to fly through the water, diving and turning with great agility, even though it has a rigid body. The lower part of the shell has a hingelike joint, allowing the turtle to breathe deeply for long dives. The nostrils are at the tip of the nose, enabling the animal to breathe by only barely breaking the water's surface. A marine turtle's size is impressive; some measure as long as 7 feet (2.1 meters).

Spending almost their entire lives at sea, marine turtles come onto land only briefly. At the start of the nesting season, turtles gather in the waters just off their traditional nesting beaches. Mating takes place in the sea. Eventually the females swim ashore and begin the slow, laborious progress up the beach to the soft sand just above the tide line. Here they dig their nests and lay their round, white eggs.

Each female lays about a hundred eggs before filling in the nest with sand and returning to the sea. If all goes well and the nest is not disturbed by predators, the eggs, warmed by the sun, hatch in a few weeks. The young turtles struggle to the surface and instinctively move toward the ocean. During

their dash to the water, they may fall victim to crabs by night or seabirds by day. Once in the water, they may be taken by sharks and other hungry fish.

Few survive this difficult time, but enough make it into deep water to perpetuate the species, and after years of feeding and growing at sea, each turtle returns to the beach of its birth to complete the cycle.

Turtles have few natural enemies once they reach full size. Some bear the scars of shark attack, but apart from this danger, the turtle's size and thick shell, along with its speed and diving ability, provide excellent protection against predators. However, the turtle's worst enemy is humankind. Thousands are killed each year for their shells and for use as food.

Although turtles may be protected in some places, they cover wide areas and may be hunted in other parts of their range. There is a real danger of the total extinction of some species. In common with many other giants of the sea, the future of the turtle will be determined by humans. The problem is known, and the solutions are clear. All that is lacking at present is the will to achieve the best results.

Hawksbill turtles range throughout the warmer oceans of the world. Like other marine turtles, the long limbs allow them to swim gracefully through the water in a seemingly effortless manner.

A green sea turtle hatchling finally reaches the water after its long, dangerous journey from its birthplace on the beach. With luck, it will be one of the few of its generation to survive, grow to adulthood, and perpetuate its species.

INDEX

*Page numbers in **bold-face** type indicate photo captions.*